DRUGS **the facts about**
LSD **AND OTHER**
HALLUCINOGENS

DRUGS the facts about
LSD AND OTHER HALLUCINOGENS

SUZANNE LEVERT

Marshall Cavendish
Benchmark
New York

Series Consultant: Dr. Amy Kohn, Chief Executive Officer, YWCA of White Plains and Central Westchester, New York.
Thanks to John M. Roll, Ph.D., Director of Behavioral Pharmacology at UCLA Integrated Substance Abuse Programs, for his expert reading of this manuscript.

Marshall Cavendish Benchmark
99 White Plains Road
Tarrytown, NY 10591
www.marshallcavendish.us

Library of Congress Cataloging-in-Publication Data
LeVert, Suzanne.
The facts about LSD and other hallucinogens / by Suzanne LeVert.
p. cm. — (Drugs)
Summary: "Describes the history, characteristics, legal status, and abuse of LSD"—Provided by publisher.
Includes bibliographical references and index.
ISBN 0-7614-1974-8
1. LSD (Drug)—Juvenile literature. I. Title. II. Series: Drugs (Marshall Cavendish Benchmark (Firm))
RM666.L88L485 2005
615'.7883—dc22
2005003948

Photo research by Joan Meisel

Cover photo: Royalty-Free/Corbis

Alamy: David Hoffman Photo Library, 6; Stephen Shepherd, 74. Corbis: Royalty-Free, 1, 2-3, 5; Bettmann, 17, 20, 67; Ted Streshinsky, 19, 34; Minnesota Historical Society, 62; James Leynse, 85. Getty Images: Hulton Archive, 13. Peter Arnold, Inc.: David Cavagnaro, 48. Photo Researchers, Inc.: George Post, 8; SPL, 26, 30; Mehau Kulyk/Science Photo Library. 37; Alfred Pasieka/Science Photo Library, 39; David Gifford/Science Photo Library, 41.

Printed in China

1 3 5 6 4 2

CONTENTS

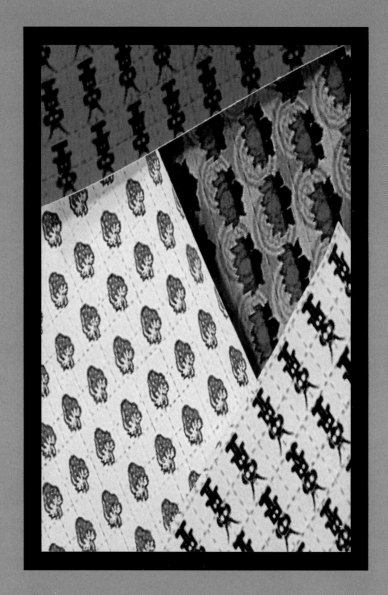

LSD IS MOST OFTEN USED IN BLOTTER PAPER FORM. FULL SHEETS OF THE PAPER ARE DECORATED WITH ARTWORK OR DESIGNS, PERFORATED, THEN SOAKED IN LIQUID LSD SOLUTION AND DRIED. EACH SMALL SQUARE CONTAINS A SINGLE DOSE.

1 What Is LSD?

LYSERGIC ACID DIETHYLAMIDE (LSD), commonly known as acid, is a member of a class of drugs called hallucinogens or psychedelics. Used for centuries as a gateway to religious, spiritual, and psychological growth by many communities throughout the world, hallucinogens alter the functioning of the brain and often create artificial perceptions. LSD is the most common hallucinogen and also one of the most potent. It only takes a tiny amount of the drug to bring about a powerful experience, known as a "trip," that can last up to twelve hours.

Hallucinogens are drugs that cause altered states of perception and feeling. They sometimes produce flashbacks, which are episodes that occur well after

PEYOTE CACTUSES CONTAIN THE HALLUCINOGENIC DRUG MESCALINE. NATIVE AMERICANS HAVE USED PEYOTE IN TRADITIONAL CEREMONIES FOR THOUSANDS OF YEARS.

the initial effects of LSD wear off, in which part of the LSD-induced trip recurs in the mind of the user. There are two types of hallucinogens. Those that are derived from natural sources, plants such as the peyote cactus and psilocybin-containing mushrooms, and those that are chemically manufactured, such as LSD, MDMA (Ecstasy), and PCP, among others.

Hallucinogens have powerful mind-altering effects. They can change how the brain perceives time, everyday reality, and the surrounding environment. They affect regions and structures in the brain that are responsible for coordination, thought processes, hearing, and sight. They can cause people who use them to hear voices, see images, and feel sensations that do not exist. Researchers are not certain if brain chemistry permanently changes as a result of hallucinogen use, but some people who use certain of these substances appear to develop chronic mental disorders.

LSD and other hallucinogens became particularly popular in the United States in the 1960s. During that decade, a so-called drug culture emerged, led by controversial Harvard professor, Timothy Leary, along with popular musicians such as Jimi Hendrix and John Lennon, and political activists such as Abbie Hoffman. This culture mingled drugs with music, politics, and social change.

Changes in the law and changes in public opinion about drug use and other social issues contributed to a decline in LSD use in the 1970s and 1980s.

The 1990s, however, brought a resurgence of LSD use when, once again, LSD became linked to a social movement and a musical style—when all-night "rave" parties became popular among teenagers and young adults. The rave culture persists today among millions of youth, combining club and techno music with the use of LSD and other hallucinogens, including Ecstasy and mushroom-derived substances.

The History of LSD

For centuries, artists have used hallucinogens to foster inspiration, physicians have prescribed them as medicine, psychologists have provided them to patients in hopes of furthering therapy, and practitioners of certain religions have used them as tools of spiritual growth.

Archaeological evidence places the first use of hallucinogenic substances between 7,000 and 9,000 years ago. The Hindu holy book, *Rig Veda*, mentions *soma*, a sacred substance used to induce higher levels of consciousness. The ancient Aztecs used something called *teotlaqualli* in ceremonies. This was a paste made from the hallucinogenic plant, *ololiuqui*. The paste was rubbed on the skin of Aztec priests and soldiers, and was supposed to eliminate fear and to prepare the user to serve the Aztec gods. Native Americans learned of peyote, a mescaline-containing hallucinogen, from Mexican Indians and began using it in certain rituals. The Native

Street Names for LSD and Other Hallucinogens

LSD
acid
blotter
dots
mellow yellow
windowpane

PCP
angel dust
boat
elephant tranquilizers
killer weed
rocket fuel
tic tac
zoom

Psilocybin
magic mushrooms
musk
shrome

American Church still uses peyote in religious ceremonies. Some historians argue that hallucinogens
may have caused the bizarre behavior of women
who were accused of being witches in the Salem,
Massachusetts, witch trials.

LSD Discovered

The origins of LSD can be traced to a Swiss laboratory called Sandoz, which invested heavily in finding
new drugs for medical purposes. In the mid-1930s,
Sandoz concentrated much of its research on ergot,
a type of fungus that grows on diseased kernels
of rye, long known as a folk remedy. One scientist,
Albert Hofmann, began synthesizing molecules of
ergot and testing it on animals to see if it could be
used to treat any number of illnesses, including
migraine. In 1943 Hofmann isolated LSD and took it
himself as an experiment.

Within forty minutes after taking the drug,
Hofmann was dizzy and exhilarated. He later
reported that everything he saw and heard was distorted and unreal. "The dizziness and sensation of
fainting became so strong at times that I could no
longer hold myself erect . . . ," Hofmann wrote in his
1963 memoir, *LSD: My Problem Child.* "My surrounding had now transformed themselves in more terri-
fying ways. Everything in the room spun around,
and the familiar objects and pieces of furniture
assumed grotesque threatening forms."

ALBERT HOFMANN SYNTHESIZED LSD FOR THE FIRST TIME IN 1938. ON APRIL 16, 1943, HOFMANN WAS THE FIRST HUMAN TO EXPERIENCE THE EFFECTS OF LSD AFTER HE ACCIDENTALLY INGESTED A SMALL AMOUNT.

Soon, other scientists were testing the drug on both animals and humans. In humans, low doses of the drug appeared to release suppressed memories—memories of events or feelings the user had never remembered before—leading many psychiatrists and psychologists to believe that LSD could be a valuable tool in psychotherapy. In fact, during the 1950s, many psychologists used very low doses of LSD to relax their patients and to help them explore their feelings and memories. Others used it to treat alcoholism and drug addiction.

The CIA, the Military, and LSD

With the rise of the Soviet Union and other communist governments after World War II, the United States intelligence community and military became concerned about the use of chemical and biological agents by these powers. The Central Intelligence Agency (CIA) in particular, considered LSD to be a potential psychological tool and weapon. The intelligence community conducted studies using LSD during the 1950s. These tests were designed to determine the potential effects of chemical or biological agents against individuals unaware that they had received a drug. These testing programs were considered highly sensitive by the intelligence agencies administering them. Few people, even those within the agencies, knew of the programs, and there is no evidence that either the executive branch or Congress was ever informed of them.

One highly secret project—known as MKULTRA—used physicians, toxicologists, and other specialists in hospitals and prisons to conduct intensive tests on human subjects with LSD and other drugs. As recorded in a report prepared for a congressional committee investigating the CIA's mind control experiments (*Project MKULTRA: The CIA's Program of Research in Behavioral Modification*, 1977), the goals of the MKULTRA project included developing the following:

- Substances that promote illogical thinking and impulsiveness to the point where the recipient would be discredited in public;
- Materials to render the induction of hypnosis easier—substances that produce "pure" euphoria with no subsequent letdown;
- Materials and physical methods that produce amnesia for events preceding and during their use;
- Substances that alter personality structure in such a way that the tendency of the recipient to become dependent upon another person is enhanced; and
- Substances that lower the ambition and general working efficiency of men.

According to the 1977 report, which was created by a Senate Select Committee on Intelligence, one of the first studies was conducted by the National

Institute of Mental Health (NIMH) Addiction Research Center in Lexington, Kentucky, a prison for drug abusers serving sentences for drug violations. Physicians there tested volunteers among the prisoners who, after taking a brief physical examination and signing a general consent form, were administered hallucinogenic drugs. As a reward for participation in the program, the addicts were provided with the drug to which they were addicted. In a separate phase of the program, the CIA administered LSD to unwitting nonvolunteers in order to discover how people would react in "operational settings." They did so using subjects both here in the United States and abroad.

LSD was tested not only by the CIA during this period, but also by the United States Army. According to the 1977 Senate Select Committee on Intelligence, there were three major phases in the Army's testing of LSD. In the first phase, LSD was administered to more than a thousand American soldiers who volunteered to be subjects in chemical warfare experiments. In the second phase, ninety-five volunteers received LSD in clinical experiments designed to evaluate potential intelligence uses of the drug. In the third phase, sixteen unwitting nonvolunteer subjects were interrogated after receiving LSD as part of operational field tests.

The testing of unwilling and unwitting subjects was in direct violation of their civil rights, and it put hundreds of people at medical and psychological

PRESIDENT GERALD FORD MEETS WITH THE FAMILY OF DR. FRANK OLSON. THE PRESIDENT APOLOGIZED ON BEHALF OF THE U.S. GOVERNMENT FOR DR. OLSON'S SUICIDE, WHICH OCCURRED WHEN HE WAS SECRETLY GIVEN LSD BY THE CIA AS PART OF AN EXPERIMENT.

risk. One of the most tragic and well-known results of this testing was the death of Dr. Frank Olson, a civilian employee of the Army, who died on November 27, 1953. Olson unwittingly received approximately 70 micrograms of LSD in a glass of Cointreau (liqueur) that he drank on November 19, 1953. The drug had been placed in the bottle by two CIA physicians as part of an experiment at a meeting of Army and CIA scientists.

Shortly after receiving this dose of LSD, Olson exhibited symptoms of paranoia and schizophrenia.

Accompanied by one of the CIA physicians, Olson sought psychiatric assistance in New York City from another doctor whose research on LSD had been funded indirectly by the CIA. While in New York for treatment, Olson fell to his death from a tenth-story hotel window.

Despite the case of Dr. Olson, testing with LSD and other hallucinogens by the CIA and the military continued until at least 1963 and remains a stain on the record of the United States government.

The Psychedelic Era

Quite separate from the secret military experiments was a boom in LSD use by adults and youth throughout the United States, especially on college and university campuses. In particular, two Harvard University professors, Timothy Leary and Richard Alpert, began to promote the use of the drug during the early 1960s. They developed a new field, called psychedelic research, which explored the use of the drug. Leary and Alpert lost their Harvard teaching positions in 1963. Ken Kesey, a West Coast author, became another spokesman for the benefits of LSD. Kesey was a young author who had written the highly praised novel, *One Flew Over the Cuckoo's Nest*. He and a group of cohorts nicknamed "The Merry Pranksters" toured the West Coast of the United States, performing "tests" of the drug at parties. Journalist Tom Wolfe chronicled these events in

IN 1964, NOVELIST KEN KESEY STARTED A JOURNEY ACROSS THE UNITED STATES IN A PSYCHEDELIC SCHOOL BUS WITH A GROUP OF PEOPLE WHO CALLED THEM- SELVES THE MERRY PRANKSTERS. AT EACH STOP ALONG THE WAY, KESEY HOSTED FESTIVALS CALLED ACID TESTS THAT FEATURED LSD AND LIVE MUSIC.

his nonfiction novel *The Electric Kool-Aid Acid Test*, published in 1968.

At the same time, the United States was undergoing a dramatic time of social and political upheaval. Politically, the nation was in turmoil over U.S. involvement in the Vietnam War, and demonstrations about that involvement, some of them violent, were common across the country. The civil rights movement, which advocated

TIMOTHY LEARY WAS AN AMERICAN WRITER AND PSYCHOLOGIST WHO IS BEST KNOWN FOR HIS ADVOCACY OF LSD USE AND PARTICIPATION IN THE PSYCHEDELIC MOVEMENT DURING THE 1960S.

equal rights for African Americans and other minorities, also divided the country. Rock-and-roll music, and its cousin, soul music, spoke of these issues in ways that attracted and united many young people in this era of change. Until 1966 LSD was still legal, in plentiful supply, and very popular among young people who had "tuned in" to rock-and-roll and soul music and "turned on" to drugs. So too were other hallucinogens, including mushrooms that contained the hallucinogen psilocybin, and mescaline, a chemical derived from the peyote cactus.

In addition, increasing numbers of psychologists and psychiatrists were studying LSD, hoping that the drug would help their patients during therapy. Two doctors in particular, Dr. Oscar Janiger and Dr. Sidney Cohen of Los Angeles, administered LSD to many of their patients in order to study the drug's effects on creativity and insight. Experiments included providing patients who were also artists with canvases upon which to draw or paint during their LSD trip.

Such tests proved inconclusive at best for at least two reasons: Creativity itself is difficult to measure or quantify, so LSD's effects on the process were impossible to determine. And LSD appears to affect each person who takes it in a different way, and each "batch" of LSD manufactured may have a different chemical makeup and thus trigger unique changes in the brain.

By the early 1970s, LSD's popularity had waned. News stories—some of them true and some of them not—began to emerge about the dangers of LSD use. From the early 1970s until the mid-1990s, use of the drug steadily declined until rave parties fostered a new drug culture among the youth of America.

Tripping: LSD Effects

It takes only a minuscule amount of LSD to trigger reactions in the brain. In fact, dosages of LSD are measured in micrograms, or millionths of a gram. About half an hour after taking a dose, or "hit," of LSD, the drug begins to take effect in the brain. It usually takes about four to six hours for these effects to peak, and it isn't until twelve to fourteen hours later that the effects fade away.

Although body temperature often rises slightly and the pupils of the eyes dilate, the experience of an LSD trip is mostly psychological. Most users perceive distorted shapes and intense colors, and—as its placement as a hallucinogen implies—experience hallucinations that include changes in hearing and awareness of time and place. LSD users usually know that these changes in perception are temporary, but they nevertheless can become upset and confused. LSD also acts on certain types of nervous system pathways in the brain that help to regulate mood, pain, perception, personality, sexual activity, and other functions.

"I first took LSD at a rave when I was fifteen years old," Jeremy, now eighteen, admits.

> A friend of mine gave it to me. I didn't really know what I was taking, and probably, had I known what it was, I would have passed. I kinda thought it was going to be like Ecstasy, which I'd taken once before and which mellowed me out and made me feel warm, but it didn't make me see things. I wasn't prepared at all for what happened to me. Thank goodness I was with friends who knew what was going on.

Jeremy remembers feeling dizzy, then beginning to see familiar objects change shape before him.

> My buddy's backpack started morphing into a monkey that was riding on him piggyback. I thought it was hilarious. Colors changed, became more vivid and fluid. Things looked like they were melting. At first it was really cool, but after a while, everyone's speaking voice began to sound distorted and I got scared—more and more scared as the night went on. I was shaking a little, and I started sweating a lot. I didn't know what was happening. My friends took me to a quiet room in the house and sat with me. After about two hours, I guess, the hallucinations started tapering off and I was okay. But for awhile there . . . Well, I know that some people think LSD is a really cool trip, but I don't think I'll ever do it again. I didn't like feeling out of control of my mind and perceptions.

A "bad trip" on LSD can cause feelings of anxiety and paranoia, along with physical symptoms such as increased blood pressure and heart rate, and chills and muscle weakness. There are no documented fatalities from LSD, and no known toxic or fatal dose, but fatal accidents and suicides have occurred. Although hallucinogens are not usually toxic to the human body or brain, the psychological effects can sometimes lead to serious injury or death. Therefore, the drug remains dangerous, even though tolerance (needing more of the drug to achieve the same effects) and addiction (urgent physical or psychological need for a substance) are rare.

Nevertheless, the one thing upon which all researchers agree—even those who believe that the laws banning all LSD use should be changed—is that LSD is highly unpredictable. The same dose can trigger very different reactions in different people, and even in the same person on a different day or in a different mood.

Other Hallucinogens

LSD is just one of a number of hallucinogens that are used illegally for recreational purposes in the United States today.

Lysergamides

There are two types of lysergamides: LSD and lysergic acid hydroxyethylamide, a naturally occurring hallucinogen found in certain plants. The seeds of several species of morning glory (*Ipomoea violacea*) and Hawaiian woodrose (*Argyreia nervosa*) contain lysergic acid hydroxyethylamide, which has approximately one tenth the potency of LSD.

Phenylethylamines

Phenylethylamines, also called hallucinogenic amphetamines, cause not only hallucinations and changes in perception, but also have effects similar to those of amphetamines. Amphetamines are a class of drugs that speed up body processes, including heart rate and blood pressure, leading to feelings of alertness and agitation.

Mescaline is the psychogenic amphetamine found in the peyote cactus, *Lophophora williamsii*, which has been used by Native Americans for more than 8,000 years. Even today, by law, members of the Native American Church are still permitted to use the drug in religious ceremonies. Mescaline also may be sold as pills containing ground peyote.

MDMA (Ecstasy) is an artificial drug structurally similar to mescaline and amphetamines. It was developed by illegal drug traffickers in order to avoid government prosecution under drug laws that ban LSD and mescaline. First synthesized in 1914, MDMA is presently the drug of choice at raves, in North America and Europe. It causes

MDMA, or Ecstasy, is a hallucinogenic amphetamine, acting both as a stimulant and a hallucinogen.

changes in mood and perceptions, and sometimes hallucinations.

Piperidines

Derivatives of a substance found in the black pepper plant (*Piper nigrum*), these substances are manufactured and used illegally. They produce hallucinations, but, unlike LSD and MDMA, they have severe and immediate side effects that can be deadly.

Phencyclidine, commonly known as PCP, was developed in the late 1950s as a painkiller marketed under the brand name Sernylan. The manufacturer soon withdrew the product due to reports of severe adverse psychological reactions, including extreme mood changes, agitation, and psychotic behavior. Used in veterinary medicine in the 1960s, it then became a popular drug of abuse, first observed in San Francisco. Although its ill effects became known by users, dealers often pawned off PCP as mescaline, LSD, or amphetamines to unwitting buyers. Use peaked in the late 1970s, declined in the 1980s, but made a resurgence in the 1990s.

Ketamine, structurally similar to PCP, is currently a widely used anesthetic. Abused since the 1970s, ketamine today is used largely as a club drug by young people attending raves and other dance parties. Effects can range from rapture to paranoia to boredom. The user feels its hallucinogenic effects

and experiences impaired perception. Ketamine commonly elicits an out-of-body or near-death experience; it can render the user comatose. Some street names for ketamine are K, ket, special K, vitamin K, vit K, kit kat, keller, kelly's day, green, blind squid, cat valium, purple, special la coke, super acid, and super C. Slang for experiences related to ketamine or effects of ketamine include, K-hole, K-land, baby food, and god.

Indolealkylamines
This group includes two hallucinogens derived from mushrooms, psilocybin and psilocin, and the substance known as bufotenine.

Psilocybin is found in three types of mushrooms: *Psilocybin*, *Conocybe*, and *Panaeolus*. Often growing on cow dung, these mushrooms are found in tropical regions. The effects of psilocybin last approximately four to six hours. Hallucinations are common. The mushrooms cause fewer adverse reactions than LSD, although cases of hyperthermia, seizures, and coma have been reported. Misidentification of the mushrooms in the wild and on the street is common; only one-third of "magic mushrooms" bought on the street contain psilocybin. Many are simply store-bought mushrooms laced with PCP.

Bufotenine comes from the venom of certain toads. Members of the genus *Bufo*, particularly *Bufo marinus* and *Bufo alvarius*, contain bufotenine. The toads are either licked or milked for their venom, which may then be ingested or smoked. Their dried skin also may be smoked.

Cannabinols
Marijuana is the leaf or flower of the plant *Cannabis sativa* and is commonly known as pot, grass, or weed. It contains the psychoactive substance tetrahydrocannabinol, or THC. Although usually grouped with other hallucinogens, marijuana rarely causes hallucinations. Acute effects from smoking marijuana include an alteration in perception or mood, laughing, increased appetite, and irregular heartbeat.

LSD Use Today
Although the use of LSD and other hallucinogens peaked among all age groups during the 1960s and 1970s and has fallen ever since, interest in and use of the drug emerged again during the 1990s as part of rave culture. In fact, by about 1999, one out of every six college students reported some use of hallucinogens, including LSD, mushrooms, or MDMA.

Now in its thirtieth year, Monitoring the Future (MTF) is a study performed by the University of Michigan's Institute on Social Research and funded by the National Institute on Drug Abuse. It involves surveys of more than 50,000 secondary school

MARIJUANA IS DERIVED FROM THE CANNABIS PLANT. THE DRUG IS MOST CON-CENTRATED IN THE PLANT'S FEMALE FLOWERS.

students in about 400 schools nationwide. The good news is that, according to 2004 statistics collected by the Monitoring the Future study, lifetime use of LSD fell 43 percent from 6.6 percent to 3.7 percent of all those surveyed. Since 2001 the report indicates that the annual prevalence of LSD use has declined to 0.4 percent among eighth graders, 0.6 percent among tenth graders, and 0.7 percent among twelfth graders.

The use of related illegal substances, including Ecstasy and PCP, has also fallen in recent years:

MDMA (Ecstasy). The use of Ecstasy reached an all-time high in 2001, with 5.2 percent of eighth graders, 8 percent of tenth graders, and 11.7 percent of twelfth graders surveyed admitting they used the drug at least once in their lives. Since then, levels have steadily declined and today, just 2.8 percent of eighth graders, 4.3 percent of tenth graders, and 7.5 percent of twelfth graders report ever having taken Ecstasy.

PCP. The use of this drug has been at low levels since the late 1970s and fell even lower in 2004. According to the MTF study, only 0.7 percent of teenagers surveyed report ever using PCP, down from 7 percent in 1979.

Ketamine. The annual prevalence of use among teens has been relatively low since it was first measured in 2000, and since 2002 use has steadily declined in all grade levels surveyed.

LSD Use by Students: 2004

	8TH GRADERS	10TH GRADERS	12TH GRADERS
Ever Used	1.8%	2.8%	4.6%
Used in the past year	1.1%	1.6%	2.2%
Used in the past month	0.5%	0.6%	0.7%

Other Hallucinogen Use by Students: 2004

	8TH GRADERS	10TH GRADERS	12TH GRADERS
Ever Used	3.0%	5.8%	8.7%
Used in the past year	1.9%	3.7%	5.6%
Used in the past month	0.8%	1.4%	1.7%

SOURCE: *MONITORING THE FUTURE STUDY, 2004*

Marijuana. Since a recent peak in use in 1996, the MTF study shows a decline of more than 30 percent decline in the average prevalence of use among eighth graders and a more modest decline among tenth and twelfth graders.

Despite this decline in the reported use of these potentially dangerous, sometimes lethal, substances, they remain a threat to anyone who takes them.

A WOMAN DANCES AT AN ACID TEST PARTY IN SAN FRANCISCO, 1966. THE UNPREDICTABLE EFFECTS OF LSD DEPEND ON THE DOSE, THE USER'S STATE OF MIND, AND THE SURROUNDINGS IN WHICH THE DRUG IS USED.

2 Hallucinogens and the Brain

IN HIS MEMOIR, Albert Hofmann wrote about his experimentation with LSD:

As I lay in a dazed condition with my eyes closed (I experienced daylight as disagreeably bright), there surged upon me an uninterrupted stream of fantastic images of extraordinary plasticity and vividness, accompanied by an intense kaleido-scope-like play of colors. This condition gradually passed off after three hours . . .

As far as I remember, the following were the most outstanding symptoms: vertigo; visual disturbances; the faces of those around me appeared as grotesque, colored masks; marked motoric

unrest, alternating with paralysis; an intermittent heavy feeling in the head, limbs, and the entire body, as if they were filled with lead; dry, constricted sensation in the throat; feeling of choking; clear recognition of my condition, in which state I sometimes observed, in the manner of an independent, neutral observer; that I shouted half-insanely or babbled incoherent words. Occasionally, I felt as if I were out of my body . . .

What Mr. Hofmann described occurs because the active ingredients in LSD and other hallucinogens cause certain changes in the brain and those changes trigger reactions throughout the body. These reactions involve alterations in perception as well as physiological changes to blood pressure, heart rate, and other systems.

How the Brain and Body Communicate

The human brain and nervous system dictate every human emotion, action, and physiologic function. The brain, spinal cord, and nerve fibers process and pass along information to the different parts of the body.

The brain itself is divided into several large regions, each responsible for performing certain activities. The brain stem controls such basic functions as heart rate and respiration. The cerebral cortex is the largest and most highly developed portion of the brain. Divided into four

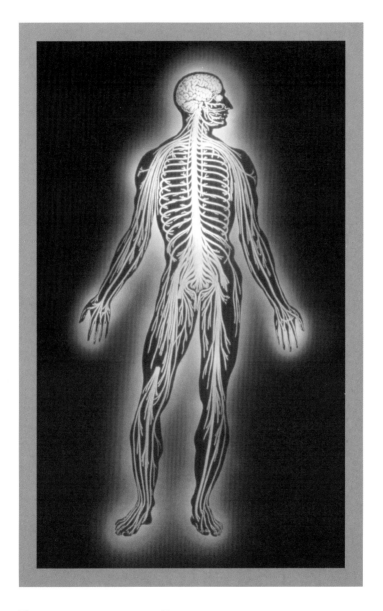

THE HUMAN NERVOUS SYSTEM. THE BRAIN AND SPINAL CORD MAKE UP THE CENTRAL NERVOUS SYSTEM, OR **CNS.** THIRTY-ONE PAIRS OF NERVES CARRY IMPULSES FROM THE SPINAL CORD OUT TO VARIOUS PARTS OF THE BODY AND BACK TO THE **CNS.**

lobes, the cortex is the center of the brain's higher powers, where the activities we define as "thinking"—thought, perception, memory, and communication—take place.

In order for these functions to occur, brain cells must be able to communicate with one another, to send messages from one cell to another, from one center of brain activity to the next. Drugs like LSD and other hallucinogens interfere with, and may even permanently alter, this communication network.

To understand how the nervous system works, scientists study not only the anatomy of the brain—its large structures and organization—but also the biochemical processes that take place among the tiniest cells of the nervous system, called neurons.

Each neuron is made up of three important parts: the central body, the dendrites, and the axon. Messages from other neurons enter the cell body through the dendrites, which are branchlike projections that extend from the cell body. Once the central body processes the messages, it can pass on the information to its neighboring neuron through a cablelike fiber called the axon. At speeds faster than you can imagine, information about every aspect of human physiology, emotion, and thought zips through the body from one neuron to another in precisely this manner.

But the axon of one neuron does not attach directly to its neighboring neuron. Instead, a tiny

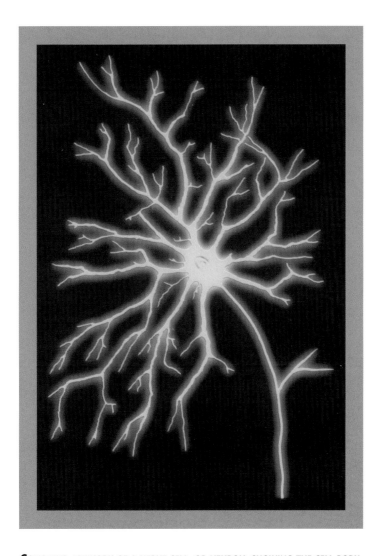

COMPUTER ARTWORK OF A NERVE CELL, OR NEURON, SHOWING THE CELL BODY, DENDRITES BRANCHING FROM THE CELL BODY, AND THE AXON (LOWER RIGHT).

gap—called a synapse—separates them. For a message to cross a synapse, it requires the help of natural chemicals called neurotransmitters, which are stored in packets at the end of each nerve cell.

When a cell is ready to send a message, its axon releases a certain amount and type of neurotransmitter. This chemical then travels across the synapse to bind to special molecules, called receptors, which sit on the surfaces of all cells in the body and bind to specific chemicals. Receptors are very complex structures. They have sites into which a very specific neurotransmitter molecule can fit. This arrangement is much like a lock-and-key mechanism. The neurotransmitter molecules from the first molecule are the keys, and the receptors on the second molecule are the locks. When the key enters the lock by binding to the receptor molecule, the lock operates and the transmission of the message is complete.

Within a fraction of a second after one neuron sends the next neuron its message, the neurotransmitter involved withdraws from the synapse into the neurons in a process called reuptake. In the presence of certain drugs, including hallucinogens, this reuptake process fails, leaving abnormally high level of neurotransmitters in the synapses.

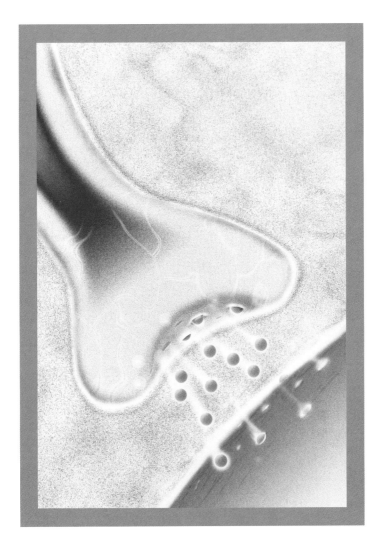

THIS ILLUSTRATION SHOWS A SYNAPSE BETWEEN TWO NERVE CELLS. NERVE "MESSAGES" ARE CARRIED ACROSS THE SYNAPSE BY NEUROTRANSMITTERS IN TINY SPHERES (SHOWN IN ORANGE).

41

How Hallucinogens Affect the Brain

Serotonin is a chemical in the brain that influences feelings, behaviors, and body processes. Some of the important functions linked to serotonin activity include appetite, sleep, mood, and sexual drive. A group of cells in the brain stem produce serotonin from an amino acid called L-tryptophan. Cells in the digestive system and certain skin and blood cells also create serotonin. Scientists have identified more than a dozen different kinds of serotonin receptors in different areas of the body.

Dopamine is another brain chemical that affects a number of physical and psychological functions, including memory, attention, and movement. It also plays a key role in motivation, pleasure, and addiction. The brain has a network of nerve cells that produce and/or respond to dopamine. The effects of dopamine depend on where it is released, how much is released, and which type of dopamine receptors are activated. Many physical and mental disorders involve too much or too little dopamine. Hallucinogens and other illicit drugs affect dopamine pathways.

Glutamate is one of the most plentiful neurotransmitters in the brain. It acts as an "excitatory transmitter," which means that it helps the initiation of a nerve impulse in the receiving neuron, thereby aiding in the transmission of messages. It does so primarily in the cerebral cortex and limbic system, which are the parts of the brain responsible for thought processes and emotions. Scientists believe that the glutamate system in the brain is involved in many facets of addiction, including anticipation, reward, tolerance, and dependence.

According to current research, LSD prevents the reuptake of serotonin. Although found throughout the brain, serotonin primarily concentrates in two parts of the brain: the cerebral cortex and the locus coeruleus. The cerebral cortex controls thought, mood, and perception, so an imbalance of serotonin in this area of the brain causes changes in those areas. The locus coeruleus, on the other hand, receives and translates sensory signals. Therefore, an imbalance of serotonin in this area of the brain often leads to bizarre sensory experiences, including auditory, visual, and tactile hallucinations.

Both the sensory and physiological effects of LSD are temporary. Long-term studies have shown that no permanent damage to the brain takes place, even with repeated use. Furthermore, the active substances in LSD do not appear to be toxic to the body, at least not in the amounts usually taken. However, injuries and deaths of LSD users may occur because of often reckless behavior triggered by effects of the drug.

Other members of the hallucinogenic family of drugs have similar effects, but some appear to pose special risks.

Julie, a seventeen-year-old high school senior, started experimenting with drugs when she was a freshman.

I was your typical rebel—breaking all the rules as soon as I hit the high school doors. I started smoking ciga-rettes, then marijuana. I drank and partied. A couple friends of mine were into doing Ecstasy and LSD on the weekends, so I tried it with them. I loved what it did to reality—pushed it out of the way, changed it. At first it was scary because, once you take LSD, there's no telling what you'll see or feel or hear, and there's no way to stop the trip once you're on it. I probably did it five or six times in the three years I was into drugs.

Julie admits she was lucky when it came to her experimentation with LSD.

I didn't have any bad trips, I never got out of control or did anything stupid. But an acquaintance of mine did. She thought she could drive a car while on acid—a stupid thing to do, but when reality gets distorted, so does your judgment. She got into a terrible acci-dent. She nearly died. That kind of shook me up. So did seeing that I wasn't going to get anywhere doing all these drugs and not doing school work and getting in trouble all the time with my parents. I went into rehab for thirty days and kicked everything, including drinking. I feel better now, and I'd never risk my health again by taking LSD or any other drug.

Mescaline primarily affects the activity of serotonin by blocking its reuptake into the neurons that released them. It affects each individual who uses it in a different way. Although mescaline is best known for its ability to trigger hallucinations, it also has physiological effects, including increased heart rate and blood pressure.

MDMA (Ecstasy) triggers an imbalance of both serotonin and dopamine. Particularly alarming is research on animals that has demonstrated that MDMA can damage and destroy serotonin-containing neurons. This damage may produce harmful effects on mood, thoughts, sleep, and motivation. MDMA can cause hallucinations, confusion, depression, sleep problems, severe anxiety, and paranoia.

PCP affects many neurotransmitter systems. It interferes with the functioning of the neurotransmitter glutamate, which is found in neurons throughout the brain. Like many other drugs, it also causes dopamine to be released from neurons into the synapse. At low to moderate doses, PCP causes altered perception of body image, but rarely produces visual hallucinations. PCP can also cause effects that mimic the primary symptoms of schizophrenia, such as delusions and mental turmoil. People who use PCP for long periods of time may end up with permanent memory loss and speech difficulties.

Ketamine is an anesthetic legal in this country only as an animal tranquilizer. Like PCP, ketamine interferes with the activity of the neurotransmitter glutamate. It mainly binds to and blocks glutamate receptors all over the brain and changes the way cells integrate or interpret incoming data. Doctors do not believe that ketamine is addictive, but users may develop a tolerance for it, which means they must take higher doses to achieve the same results they have experienced in the past. This need for greater doses of the drug could pose a serious risk of overdose, particularly because of the unpredictability of the drug's effects.

Is LSD Addictive?

Since the advent of LSD in the 1950s, scientists have questioned whether or not LSD is an addictive substance. To date, there is no evidence that people who take LSD over a prolonged period of time develop physiological or psychological dependence on the drug. For one thing, unlike shorter-acting substances such as cocaine or even marijuana, hallucinogens have effects that last for several hours. Users have reported feeling exhausted and spent after a trip on LSD, which quells the urge to take the drug many times a day. The uncertain and mixed effects of LSD lead to erratic instances of its use. And extremely powerful and intense hallucinations often prompt users

46

to abstain from using LSD, especially after experiencing a bad trip.

Although the risks of developing tolerance for or dependence on LSD appears to be minimal, there are some serious health risks associated with taking the drug.

THE ERGOT FUNGUS, WHICH INFECTS RYE AND OTHER RELATED GRASSES, HAS LONG BEEN USED IN PRESCRIPTION DRUGS TO TREAT VARIOUS AILMENTS, INCLUDING MIGRAINE HEADACHES. LSD IS SYNTHESIZED BY COMBINING LYSERGIC ACID, WHICH OCCURS NATURALLY IN THE ERGOT FUNGUS, WITH DIETHYLAMIDE.

3 Psychedelic Risks

LSD IS THE MOST potent mood- and perception-altering drug known: oral doses as small as 30 micrograms can produce effects that last from six to twelve hours, and sometimes longer. LSD is produced by a relatively small number of drug makers, most of them working out of small, secret labs, primarily on the West Coast of the United States.

LSD is produced from lysergic acid, which is derived from the tartrate salt of ergotamine, which comes from the ergot fungus on rye. Only a small amount of ergotamine tartrate is required to produce LSD in large batches.

Manufacturing is time-consuming and dangerous. It takes from two to three days to produce about 50 grams of pure LSD crystals. Some of the chemical reactions involved in the process may cause explosions if not performed by a trained chemist.

The pure crystal can be crushed to powder and mixed with binding agents to produce pills known as "microdots" or thin squares of gelatin called "windowpanes." Usually, however, distributors dissolve and dilute it, then apply it to paper or other materials. This is called blotter acid. These sheets of LSD-soaked paper are perforated into 1/4-inch square, individual dosage units.

Although the original LSD crystals are usually white, variations in manufacturing and the presence of contaminants causes variations in the color of the finished product, which can range from clear or white to tan or even black. Even uncontaminated LSD begins to degrade and discolor soon after it is manufactured, and drug distributors often apply LSD to colored paper, making it difficult for a buyer to determine the drug's purity or age.

Because LSD is not subject to any controls over its manufacturing process as are legal drugs, there is no way of knowing how strong a particular dose of the drug is, nor what is in it. Although statistics indicate that a typical dose of LSD sold in the 1960s was about 300 micrograms compared to today's average dose of about 20 to 80 micrograms, a user's reactions to LSD remain unpredictable because of this lack of control over its manufacture.

"Dropping acid," as taking LSD is known among users, usually consists of a user chewing and swallowing a tab of blotter acid. The body then digests the paper, and the gastrointestinal tract and the mucus

Forms of LSD

Name	Form
Microdots	Tiny LSD-containing pills users swallow
Windowpane	Small, thin sheets of gelatin cut into tiny squares
Sugar cubes	Cubes of sugar containing liquid LSD
Blotted paper	The most popular form of LSD, consisting of sheets of paper soaked in LSD, then dried. Users tear off squares of the paper and lick or chew them.

membranes (the linings of body passages and cavities) absorb the LSD. Most body tissues, including the kidneys and the liver, absorb LSD quickly. Thus, only small amounts actually travel through the bloodstream to the brain, but even a minuscule amount is enough to trigger hallucinations and other effects.

How LSD Affects the Body and Brain

The effects of LSD are twofold. First, it alters users' sensory perceptions, changing the way they see, feel, hear, taste, and touch the world around them. Second, LSD affects the way the body behaves, including dilating the eyes' pupils, lowering body temperature, producing nausea, causing profuse sweating, and creating goose bumps. Less common effects include rapid heartbeat and elevated blood pressure.

By far, the first set of effects is more dramatic. Starting anywhere from twenty minutes to two hours after ingesting LSD, users may experience a

tingling sensation in their limbs. All of their senses become more acute. Many experience a heightened sexual arousal. Many users, especially those taking LSD for the first time, feel tense at first. Then, as the drug takes hold, they release their emotions by laughing or crying. Emotional reactions to the drug's effects as the trip continues are common, but varied. Moods tend to become more intense and changeable. Often, the user's underlying emotional state is exacerbated, and any underlying psychological disturbance can come to the forefront.

About two to three hours after taking LSD, users may experience visual hallucinations, such as colors becoming more intense or glowing and objects appearing to change shape. Some users start to become afraid because they feel they are losing their "sense of self," especially if they are inexperienced with the drug or have taken a higher than usual dose. An hour or so after that, users often experience an altered sense of time and of themselves. Moods often change easily and quickly through the experience. The effects of the trip may last two to six hours in some individuals. Some users experience a brief period of depression after LSD use.

Bad Trips: The Downside of LSD

While using LSD, or "tripping," the person may experience strong feelings of anxiety or fear. The hallucinatory effects can be unpleasant; for example, spiders crawling on the skin. Or they can be so intense that the person feels as though they are losing control and "going crazy." Panic can lead to risky behavior, such as running across a busy street. Paranoia, intense fear of

Effects of LSD and Other Hallucinogens

- "Seeing" vivid colors
- Hallucinations
- Emotional reactions, sometimes extreme
- Distortion of the senses and of time and space
- Increase in heart rate and blood pressure
- Chills
- Muscle weakness
- Mood swings
- Feelings of fear and paranoia
- Loss of "sense of self"

persecution, and feelings of superiority can sometimes develop. These feelings of invulnerability can cause people to injure themselves accidentally; for example, by diving into rough surf. Usually the negative feelings go away when the drug wears off. Among the strong, negative reactions to LSD are the following:

- **Paranoia and suspicion:** Users may feel that others are out to harm them or that they are in danger.
- **Superman syndrome:** Believing that they are indestructible, some LSD users will take enormous risks to themselves and others, including running into traffic, jumping out of windows, and performing other dangerous activities.

• **Depression:** LSD can trigger or increase feelings of unhappiness and low self-esteem. During a trip, these emotions can overwhelm the user and persist for hours, even after the effects of the drug have worn off. Users have been known to attempt suicide or express violent behavior toward others.

Albert Hofmann, LSD's inventor and first human subject, had his own experience with a bad trip, as he wrote in his memoir:

A demon had invaded me, had taken possession of my body, mind, and soul. I jumped up and screamed, trying to free myself from him, but then sank down again and lay helpless on the sofa. The substance, with which I had wanted to experiment, had vanquished me. . . . I was seized by the dreadful fear of going insane. I was taken to another world, another place, another time. My body seemed to be without sensation, lifeless, strange. Was I dying? Was this the transition? . . . I had not even taken leave of my family (my wife, with our three children, had traveled that day to visit her parents, in Lucerne). Would they ever understand that I had not experimented thoughtlessly, irresponsibly, but rather with the utmost caution, and that such a result was in no way foreseeable?

Because the content and strength of a dose of LSD is so unknown, and its effects so unpredictable, it is impossible to prevent a bad trip or predict its occurrence. Anecdotal evidence suggests that taking

LSD in a safe and comfortable environment, around trusted people, and in a confident and emotionally stable mood, can help make the experience better, but there is no way to predict a user's experience.

Although a bad trip does not itself cause any serious medical or psychological harm, there are dangers associated with such an experience. A user experiencing a bad trip is more likely to harm himself or herself because of the often overwhelming feelings of paranoia, anxiety, or—in some cases—invulnerability. In November 2004, the *Los Angeles Times* reported that three teenagers were arrested after allegedly giving hallucinogenic mushrooms to a Newbury Park girl who was then fatally struck by a car as she wandered naked on the Ventura Freeway.

In order to protect someone who's having a bad trip, those around that person should first make sure that he or she is safe. They should move and speak quietly and in a confident manner. In order to keep the user oriented, friends should repeat his or her name and let the tripper know where he or she is. Most important, a person experiencing a bad trip should never be left alone.

Flashbacks: Returning to the Trip

Days, weeks, or even years after using the drug, some people have a repeat experience of the effects of LSD. Called flashbacks, or HPPD (hallucinogenpersisting perception disorder), these experiences cause a user to see intense colors and other hallucinations without

Jason, a seventeen-year-old high school junior, has used LSD three or four times in the past two years.

> I wanted to see what it was like. I was reading the author Aldous Huxley, a very cool writer in the 1940s and 1950s. He was a vegetarian and a humanist, and he wrote about his experiences with LSD in a book called The Doors of Perception. In school, we were studying the politics and culture of the 1960s. . . . I just became interested in expanding the mind this way, maybe to see the world from a different angle.

Jason found it easy to buy LSD in the small Northeast city where he lives. "I go to a prep school. I asked a friend who asked a friend. It took about a day to track it down right on campus. A few tabs of acid cost me about fifteen dollars, I think." Although the supply of LSD has diminished in the United States in recent years, Jason's ease in obtaining the drug is common. However, the exact strength of the dose or what it contains remains arbitrary.

> The first time I took it, I was pretty scared. I made sure to do it with friends who'd done it before, so I felt pretty safe. At first, I didn't feel anything but a slight tingling in my body. Then, I could feel my heart starting to race a little bit, and I felt excited. Oddly, I had a weird taste of metal in my mouth, which I understand is normal. Then, a little while later, the trip really started. It's hard to explain what it was like: the scariest part was, for a second, I realized I'd lost myself. I mean, I couldn't think straight, couldn't gather my thoughts. I had to give in to the images that started flowing all around me. I found myself staring at the

CD player as a CD spun around. It changed color, it changed shape. I was fascinated by it.

Jason's trip lasted about four hours. "I felt tired afterward, a little depressed, but I was fine. I went to bed that night like normal, and woke up fine. I did it two more times, and it was interesting. I didn't see God, or anything, and it didn't change my life, but it didn't make me sick. But I'll never do it again."

The last time Jason took LSD, he was with three friends from his school.

One guy, Zach, I didn't know very well. We all took the acid at the same time. About an hour into it, Zach started to freak out. He was crying and pacing. He got really paranoid. He saw bugs crawling on the walls—which there weren't—and he started to become pretty violent, smashing a bowl that was on the table and whacking at the wall with his arm. It got worse and worse. Because most of us were tripping, too, we couldn't be much help. In fact, one guy thought it was the funniest thing, that Zach was seeing bugs.

Luckily, a guy named Mike from down the hall heard all the noise and came to see what was going on. He talked to Zach very calmly and took him to a quiet, dark room. But that didn't help either. Zach was crying and acting crazy. Mike was smart—he took Zach to an emergency room before he hurt himself. They made him stay the night and even now, he says he's not quite the same. He told me he'd been taking drugs to treat depression, so that's probably it. But that whole last experience was enough to turn me off to it. Someone could have gotten hurt, and I wasn't myself, so I couldn't help. I don't want to be in that position again.

taking any more of the drug. They may be sparked by the use of other drugs, by stress or fatigue, or—as is true most of the time—for reasons unknown. Flashbacks can be either pleasant or anxiety-producing. They last for a minute or two.

Effects and Side Effects of Other Hallucinogens

LSD is one of several hallucinogenic substances. Although the effects of these substances are similar, some have significant differences in terms of their immediate actions on the body and brain, as well as their risks for tolerance and dependence.

Mescaline. The active substance in peyote exists in the bitter, fleshy tops of the peyote cactus (called buttons). After ingesting about six to twelve buttons, the user first begins to feel effects in thirty minutes to two hours. Nausea and vomiting often occurs before the hallucinogenic effects.

Ecstasy (MDMA). The long-term effects of using MDMA remain unknown. Animal and primate studies show significant degradation of certain pathways in the brain. This has led some medical experts to warn regular MDMA users that permanent brain damage, could occur.

In addition, several deaths have been reported with MDMA use. Frequent users rapidly develop tolerance to the drug, requiring higher doses for the same effect.

PCP. The psychological and physical effects of PCP are severe. They include elevated body temperature, heart rate, and blood pressure, and bizarre and psychotic behaviors. PCP is associated with a much higher morbidity and mortality rate than other classes of hallucinogens. The effects of the drug put users in danger of hyperthermia (high body temperature causing organ damage) and kidney failure. Their violent and bizarre behavior places them at high risk for trauma. The dissociative effect of PCP use allows users to do tremendous harm to their bodies with little or no perceived pain. PCP goes by several street names, including angel dust, killer weed, elephant tranquilizer, and rocket fuel.

Ketamine. Like PCP, ketamine's effects include numbness, loss of coordination, a sense of invulnerability, muscle rigidity, aggressive/violent behavior, and slurred or blocked speech.

When It Becomes an Emergency

According to the latest data collected by the Substance Abuse and Mental Health Services Administration (SAMHSA), LSD and its cohorts, ketamine and MDMA, collectively were involved in about 8,100 hospital emergency-room visits in 2002. Most of the patients in these emergency-room visits were under age twenty-six, accounting for 68 percent of the ketamine, 75 percent of the MDMA, and 76 percent of the LSD-related emergency department visits.

As risky to one's health as taking LSD and other hallucinogens may be, there are other perils for users of these drugs. In this country, the manufacture, distribution, and possession of LSD and other hallucinogens is against the law, except under strict government supervision in the case of ketamine. Buying and using these drugs puts the user at risk for being arrested and convicted of a felony and potentially facing a prison term.

In the early twentieth century, drug use was legal in the United States and the sale of so-called patent remedies was widespread. Medicines containing opium, morphine, heroin, and cocaine were sold without restriction. All of that changed with the passage of the Pure Food and Drug Act of 1906, which regulated the manufacture and sale of medications.

4 LSD and the Law

FOR THOUSANDS of years, mystics and religious leaders, poets and artists, physicians and scientists— some of them quite famous and productive—have admitted to using hallucinogens, and even encouraged its use by others. After the discovery of LSD, many psychologists employed it as a therapeutic tool. Interest grew in expanding the mind by using chemicals that triggered hallucinations. Young and old alike thought taking it would "open their minds" to spiritual and creative growth.

Using or possessing LSD and most other hallucinogens is a felony—a serious crime that can lead to jail time or probation (court supervision) for as long as ten years, depending on the state or federal law that applies. Usually, the law sets the level of

punishment based on the amount of the drug that one possesses. Manufacturing, distributing, and selling LSD are also felonies. The penalty for these crimes can be even more severe than simply possessing or using the drug, and also depends on the amount of drugs law enforcement officials seize.

Scheduling LSD

As recently as the early 1900s, drug use was legal in the United States. During the nineteenth century, "patent medicines" (so called because some producers obtained patents for the medications) were very common. Many of the patent medicines contained not only alcohol, but also narcotics such as morphine, cocaine, and opium. Marketed as wonder cures for diseases ranging from the common cold to tuberculosis, these drugs were not only ineffective, but also dangerous and sometimes addictive.

In the early twentieth century, U.S. legislators enacted laws that required manufacturers to list all the ingredients in these patent medicines, as well as to support their claims for their effectiveness with scientific research. That legislation put an end to the patent medicine business and also set the stage for more stringent oversight by federal and state governments.

Today, drug laws in the United States are complicated, with each state having its own laws that sometimes differ from federal law. A branch of the U.S. Justice Department called the Drug Enforcement Administration (DEA) is the primary drug enforcement agency in the country. Its mission is to enforce the laws surrounding controlled substances and to bring to the justice system of the United States anyone found to be involved in the growth, manufacture, or distribution of controlled substances in this country.

Since 1966 it has been illegal to buy, sell, or make LSD in this country. In 1970 the U.S. Congress passed the Controlled Substances Act. Through this act, drugs are placed into one of five "schedules," or categories. The U.S. Food and Drug Administration (FDA), with help from the DEA and medical experts, decides what schedule a drug belongs in based on several factors, including the substance's medicinal value, its harmfulness, and its potential for abuse or addiction. Schedule I is reserved for the most dangerous drugs that have no recognized medical use, while Schedule V is the classification used for the least dangerous drugs. The act also provides ways for new drugs to be added or removed from a schedule depending on new information about the drugs.

The factors that government officials use when deciding in which schedule a drug belongs include the following:

- Its actual or relative potential for abuse.
- Scientific evidence of its pharmacological effect, if known.
- The state of current scientific knowledge regarding the drug or other substance.

- Its history and current pattern of abuse.
- The scope, duration, and significance of abuse
- What, if any, risk there is to the public health.
- Its psychic or physiological dependence liability.
- Whether the substance is an immediate precursor (a chemical required for its manufacture) of a substance already controlled under this title.

Using these criteria, the FDA evaluates each new drug that comes into use—legally or illegally—and places it within one of the five schedules. Rating drugs this way helps state and federal lawmakers decide on what penalty a person convicted of possessing, manufacturing, or distributing the drug should receive.

LSD, along with other hallucinogens such as MDMA, mescaline, and psilocybin, is a Schedule I drug. This means that the FDA has determined that these drugs have a high potential for abuse, have no accepted medical use, and lack acceptable safety for their use under medical supervision.

Should LSD Be Legal?

"I have been born again. I have been through a psychiatric experience which has completely changed me. I was horrendous. I had to face things about myself which I never admitted, which I didn't know were there. Now I know that I hurt every woman I

PSYCHIATRIST HUMPHREY OSMOND COINED THE TERM "PSYCHEDELIC." DR. OSMOND PROMOTED RESEARCH INTO THE USE OF LSD AS A POTENTIAL TREATMENT FOR PSYCHOLOGICAL AILMENTS. HIS EFFORTS WERE THWARTED BY FEDERAL REGULATIONS AND NEGATIVE PUBLICITY ASSOCIATED WITH LSD USE.

ever loved. I was an utter fake, a self-opinionated bore, a know-it-all who knew very little. I found I was hiding behind all kinds of defenses, hypocrisies, and vanities. I had to get rid of them layer by layer. The moment when your conscious meets your subconscious is a hell of a wrench. With me there came a day when I saw the light."

So wrote movie actor Cary Grant in an interview with *Life* magazine in 1959. For Mr. Grant and thousands of others, LSD proved to be a positive influence, while other users suffered ill effects, including suicide attempts and fatal accidents. Since its discovery, a controversy has raged over LSD's use as a psychiatric or spiritual tool versus the danger it poses.

While there is no evidence that LSD or other hallucinogens (with the exception of PCP) are addictive or toxic, their placement on Schedule I has made it difficult for scientists to test these benefits on humans. Many scientists and users argue that LSD should be removed from Schedule I into a less restrictive schedule so that studies on the drug under medical and scientific supervision could continue. In December 2004, the Food and Drug Administration approved a Harvard University plan to study MDMA (Ecstasy) as a treatment for anxiety in terminal cancer patients. Researchers in California are studying the effect of psilocybin, the active ingredient in hallucinogenic mushrooms, in similar patients. Both teams hope to learn whether the drugs, which can induce effusiveness and heightened awareness, will help people express and manage their fears in a therapeutic setting.

Those in favor of maintaining LSD and psilocybin as Schedule I drugs point to the hundreds of studies performed in the 1960s that yielded no conclusive results as to LSD's psychological or physical benefits. Those studies revealed how unpredictable and ultimately dangerous LSD is to many individuals who take it. To date, the government has no plans to change LSD's status.

Production and Trafficking of LSD

According to the DEA, LSD is made and sold in the United States by two main groups. The first group is located primarily in northern California and consists of chemists (commonly referred to as "cooks") and traffickers working together. They produce the majority of LSD sold in this country and are capable of distributing LSD nationwide. The second group consists of smaller, independent producers who operate out of labs throughout the country and sell only to local buyers.

Because the process of making LSD is relatively complicated, requiring knowledge of chemistry, there remain few manufacturers of the drug. LSD commonly is produced from lysergic acid. Lysergic acid and lysergic acid amide are both classified in Schedule III of the Controlled Substances Act. Ergotamine tartrate is regulated under the Chemical Diversion and Trafficking Act.

The U.S. Congress enacted the Chemical Diversion and Trafficking Act of 1988 in order to make it illegal to divert chemicals from their legal purpose to the illicit drug trade. Until this act went into effect, there were no legal controls over the sale of chemicals required to produce drugs of abuse like LSD. The Chemical Diversion and Trafficking Act of 1988 extended the concept of commodity control to those chemicals most often used for the manufacture and synthesis of drugs of abuse. With the support of the State Department, the DEA pursued the same goal on the international level. The result was the incorporation of Article 12 into the U.N. Convention Against Illicit Traffic in Narcotic Drugs and Psychotropic Substances of 1988 (the Vienna Convention). This provision established similar controls over a list of twenty-two critical chemicals commonly diverted for the production of the major drugs of abuse.

Ergotamine tartrate is not readily available in the United States. The DEA believes that most of the chemical used to illegally manufacture LSD comes from sources in Europe, Mexico, Costa Rica, and Africa. The difficulty in acquiring ergotamine tartrate may be one reason for the relatively small number of LSD manufacturers.

How does a dose of LSD get from a lab in northern California to a user at a rave? The DEA believes that LSD usually is transported by overnight delivery services, such as Federal Express or DHL, to local buyers. It is hidden in greeting cards, in videotapes or compact disks, or in articles of clothing that are mailed to a post office box established by the recipient.

According to recent statistics from the DEA, prices for LSD range from one to twelve dollars per dosage unit generally selling for five dollars per dosage unit. LSD is distributed by mail orders, creating a marketplace where sellers and buyers do not know each other. This level of anonymity makes it difficult for law enforcement to investigate trafficking. LSD has also been historically distributed at rock concerts, and more

recently at raves. Other hallucinogens are manufactured and priced in a different way.

Marketing Other Hallucinogens
LSD's cousins, PCP, MDMA, and ketamine, are also
manufactured and distributed primarily from secret
labs within the United States.

PCP. In January 1978, PCP was transferred from
Schedule III to Schedule II under the Controlled
Substances Act of 1970. It is now considered a
drug with a high potential for abuse, only a limited
medical use, and one that may lead to psychological and physical abuse. The Los Angeles area is
the primary source for the majority of PCP found
in the United States. According to the El Paso
Intelligence Center (EPIC) Clandestine Laboratory
Database, seventeen of the twenty-four PCP labo-
ratories seized throughout the United States from
1998 to 2002 were located in California. In most
cases, the manufacturers obtain the chemicals
necessary to process PCP from legitimate com-
mercial and bulk chemical companies under false
pretenses. Indeed, PCP traffickers are known
for establishing "front" companies for the sole
purpose of obtaining chemicals necessary for the
production of PCP as well as other illicit synthetic
drugs. PCP is available in pills, powder, and liquid
forms, as well as in PCP-laced cigarettes (both
tobacco and marijuana).

MDMA. MDMA is most often manufactured clandestinely in western Europe, primarily in Belgium and the Netherlands. These countries produce 80 percent of the MDMA consumed worldwide. This is primarily because of the availability of precursor and essential chemicals and international transportation hubs in this area of the world.

Ketamine. This animal tranquilizer is a Schedule III drug. Ketamine is produced commercially in a number of countries, including Belgium, China, Colombia, Germany, and the United States. Ketamine production is complicated and difficult; therefore most of the drug sold on the street is stolen from veterinarians or smuggled into the country from Mexico. According to the DEA, retail doses of ketamine can be purchased for about $20 to $100 per vial.

Mushrooms. Psilocybin mushrooms are difficult to grow and store. Suppliers of this drug usually operate independently and distribute locally. Mushrooms can vary in price, but usually sell for $20 for an eighth of an ounce and from $100 to $150 per ounce.

LSD and Crime

Statistics on local LSD arrests are difficult to find, but according to the DEA, which tracks arrests primarily for large-scale possession, manufacture, and distribution of LSD, 203 people were arrested in 2000, 95 in 2001, 41 in 2002, and only 19 in 2003.

In the first quarter of 2004, only three people were arested on federal LSD charges. In the LSD haven of San Francisco, the DEA recorded twenty arrests in 2000 versus zero in 2002.

These statistics about federal arrests confirm that LSD use has declined dramatically in recent years. One reason for this decline could be that, thanks to efforts by the DEA and other law enforcement agencies, the supply of the drug has been shut off.

In 2000, federal agents arrested two men, William Pickard and Clyde Apperson, both of California, who—agents contend—had been responsible for the majority of the LSD manufactured and sold in the United States. In fact, their arrest and subsequent conviction reduced the availability of the drug in this country by 95 percent. Agents seized more than 90 pounds (40 kilograms) of LSD and 300 pounds (135 kilograms) of LSD precursor chemicals with the ability to create an additional 28 pounds (13 kilograms) of the illicit drug. According to court testimony, Pickard and Apperson previously manufactured LSD in Santa Fe, New Mexico, where every five weeks the lab produced about 2.2 pounds (1 kilogram) of LSD, which translated into about 10 million doses that cost less than one cent a dose to produce and would sell for as much as $10 a dose.

Although LSD use has declined dramatically in the last decade or so, it remains available to, and popular with, thousands of teens across the country.

ALL-NIGHT PARTIES CALLED RAVES FEATURE ELECTRONIC DANCE MUSIC AND LIGHT SHOWS. A WIDE VARIETY OF DRUGS INCLUDING ECSTASY, KETAMINE, AND LSD, COLLECTIVELY KNOWN AS CLUB DRUGS, ARE OFTEN AVAILABLE AT RAVES.

5 Life without Illusions or Delusions

DOCTORS DO NOT CONSIDER LSD to be a physically or psychologically addictive drug. People who take the drug are not likely to build up tolerance or become dependent on it. Nevertheless, taking LSD can become a profound problem for many.

In the short-term, life stops for users who take a drug like LSD—at least for the twelve or more hours that the trip lasts. They cannot read a book, hold a regular conversation, or drive a car. There is no way to take LSD "in moderation" or to control the experience. When users take LSD, the experience overwhelms them and prevents them from doing anything other than endure the effects and side effects of the drug. In the long-term, many

who take LSD find that doing so becomes a bad habit: a behavior that hinders or harms them as it interferes with normal, everyday activity. Recognizing when a behavior has become a habit and learning to break that habit can be challenging, but the benefits of kicking a drug habit far outweigh any perceived benefits of continuing it.

Pop Culture and Hallucinogens

Young people experiment with illegal drugs such as LSD for any number of reasons. By nature, teens are risk takers. It is at this time in a person's life that he or she starts to break free from parental controls and to test the waters of his or her independence. Some teens also think that they are invincible and immortal, and thus do things that would be considered too dangerous by most adults.

Another reason that many young people take drugs may be to combat feelings of low self-esteem and unease about their place in society. The drugs seem to help for two reasons. First, the effects of the drugs may block feelings of anxiety and temporarily alter reality. Second, taking drugs, particularly hallucinogens, tends to be a social event that attracts like-minded people who share not only the drug-taking experience but also the same taste in music, clothing, and perhaps even opinions about political or community events.

In recent years, hallucinogens have come back into fashion, especially among well-educated adults and teenagers. Part of the reason for this resurgence in hallucinogenic use is the popularity of the so-called rave culture. Raves are characterized by loud techno or electronic music, a dark environment with laser lighting, pro-drug paraphernalia, and illicit drugs like LSD. Massage parlors and "cool-down" rooms are set up to deal with the side effects of some of the drugs, such as LSD and Ecstasy. Depending on how carefully security guards search people at the entrance, much of the drug sale activitiy may be conducted in the parking lot or areas outside the main venues. Most security guards are not very knowledgeable about drugs, and many are not serious about searching for them. Although the popularity of raves has waned in recent years, they do still occur and remain a prime site for the trafficking and use of hallucinogens.

Another indication of the drugs' popularity is the number of Web sites devoted to both rave music and drugs such as LSD and Ecstasy. The Internet is chock-full of information about hallucinogens. According to a March 2001 report in the *American Journal of Psychiatry*, a study found eighty-one hallucinogen-related sites. The authors of this study spent five hours visiting forty-six sites. Many of these Web sites encourage the use of hallucinogens as ways to "open the mind" and to connect with others on a more spiritual plane. They also insist that the dangers of LSD are minimal, and focus on the drug's nonaddictive quality as a positive indication. However, although it is true that LSD users tend not to become addicted to the drug,

using any illegal substance on a regular basis will almost certainly effect negative changes in their lives.

Recognizing LSD Abuse

How can you tell if a friend is using hallucinogens? Sometimes it's tough to tell. Different hallucinogens have different effects, depending on the dose and the user. However, some easy-to-spot physical signs include the following:

- Dilated pupils
- Anxiety or paranoia
- Mood swings
- Dizziness
- Irrational behavior

In addition to the physical signs of LSD use, however, drug use affects a person's family life, school performance, and involvement in other activities. Lying may become second nature to drug users: they must lie to their families and non-drug-taking friends about where they're going and what they're doing. They may turn to stealing in order to pay for their habits. School work will suffer as more time is spent at parties and trying to recover from the effects of the drugs than on homework and projects. Hobbies and activities that once held a teen's interest get put on the back burner as the culture of drugs takes hold.

In the end, the drug abuser usually ends up with very little but the drug-taking behavior and the friends he or she has made through that activity. At some point, either when the risks of the lifestyle outweigh the perceived benefits or when parents or law enforcement force the issue, drug-taking teens will face the fact that they must break the bad habit that's taken over their lives.

Getting Help

The first step in breaking any bad habit is recognizing that the behavior is having more negative than positive effects. Many teens come to this conclusion when their parents pull the plug, literally and figuratively, on certain privileges—such as watching television, borrowing the family car, or getting an allowance—until the bad behavior ceases. Other teens reach a crisis after experiencing a bad trip or seeing a friend suffer from one. Once they realize that taking drugs isn't worth the unpleasant consequences, they may be ready to stop.

However, breaking a bad habit is more difficult than simply stopping. Drugs like LSD often have a strong social component, so that teens who want to stop using also have to change their routines, find new hobbies, and even create a new circle of friends. How do drug abusers start this process? First, they must admit that taking LSD is a bad habit that they must break. Second, they must prepare for the many changes to their lives that will likely result from breaking the habit, such as making new friends, finding new activities that will fill the time they spent at raves or on a high, and repairing relationships with family members and old friends that were damaged during the period of drug use. Making these changes will require a great deal of commitment and tenacity not only on the part of the drug abusers trying to kick their habits, but also from their family and friends.

Sometimes, even with a nonphysically addicting drug like LSD, a drug abuser will need professional help in order to break his or her habit. Many behavioral treatments have been found to be effective for treating drug abuse, and if taking LSD and other drugs has become a problem in a teen's life, then this approach may be the best way to help break the cycle. Any medical problems related to the drug abuse will be addressed first in either an inpatient setting (at a hospital or drug rehabilitation center) or through an outpatient program. Recovery begins and continues with a learning process of breaking old habits, severing ties with drug-using friends, and identifying and then avoiding "triggers" that increase the desire to use LSD and other drugs.

Another psychosocial intervention is called cognitive-behavioral therapy. Such treatment is a short-term, focused approach to helping drug abusers stop using LSD or other substances. This kind of approach relies on the theory that using drugs is a learned behavior, and a therapist thus helps recovering abusers by using the same learning processes to reduce their drug use. It helps abusers recognize exactly when and where they would be most likely to use the drug and then to avoid those situations. A cognitive-behavioral therapist will also help the abuser learn to cope with the issues—such as low self-esteem or social discomfort—that may have triggered his or her interest in using drugs in the first place.

Another important aspect of recovering from any kind of drug abuse or addiction is dealing with the guilt and intense shame felt by most users. Most abusers feel shame because drug-using behavior often conflicts with their own values and morals, and many would rather continue to use the drugs than to face the truth about their behavior. Getting high becomes, in a sense, a short vacation from the intense guilt and shame associated with their lifestyles. Dealing with these painful issues takes time and trust. An experienced counselor, another recovering abuser, or trusted clergy can be of great help.

It is important to note that it takes some people several attempts at kicking the habit—and many stays at treatment centers—before they succeed. This difficulty speaks to the power of drugs, and a drug culture such as that associated with the rave movement, to alter mood. Fortunately, there are support groups that help bolster and enhance the success of behavioral and other psychological therapies.

Self-Help Programs

Nearly every community across the United States offers any number of organizations, treatment centers, and hotlines to help people quit using drugs. Some programs require people to remain at the center as inpatients—though this is rare for abusers who only use LSD because of its nonaddictive nature—while others provide outpatient counseling, which means that members attend scheduled therapy sessions but live at home as usual.

Among the resources available are what are known as "twelve-step" programs. Participating drug abusers accept their problems by learning from others like them that there is life after drug abuse. Twelve-step programs emphasize taking responsibility for behavior, making amends to others, and self-forgiveness. The first "step" of most of these programs states that, "We admitted we are powerless over drugs and our lives had become unmanageable."

All twelve-step programs follow some version of the twelve steps, including meeting regularly to discuss challenges and share successes. One of the most widely recognized characteristics of twelve-step groups is the requirement that members admit that they "have a problem." Members share their experiences, challenge successes and failures, and provide peer support for each other. Many people who have joined these groups report they found success that previously eluded them, while others, including some former members, criticize their methods.

Successful recovery programs strongly urge daily

attendance at twelve-step meetings for the first ninety days of sobriety. Individuals who successfully abstain from drugs of abuse must attend many twelve-step meetings for support and accountability. They often report that a part of them still looks for a good reason to use drugs. Twelve-step meetings are daily reminders of their powerlessness over drugs.

Unfortunately, as widespread as these organizations and programs appear to be, they are not reaching all of the young people whose lives have become unmanageable because taking drugs has become an ingrained, hard-to-break addiction. According to a study published in the September 2004 issue of the *Archives of Pediatric and Adolescent Medicine,* only 10 percent of the estimated 1.4 million American teens from twelve to seventeen years old with an illicit drug problem are receiving treatment, compared to about 20 percent of adults with a drug problem. Furthermore, the report noted that the programs offered to teens often don't address all of their needs. For example, adolescent drug users often have additional health problems and developmental needs and are more likely to be binge drug users than adults—and many established programs don't address those challenges very well.

Preventing Drug Abuse

Each year of the past decade or so there appeared to be a slight decline in drug use among teens. This is thanks, in part, to programs developed by government and private agencies that help to prevent

children and young adults from using illegal substances. Prevention programs vary widely, but usually include educating teens and families about the dangers of drug abuse. They also encourage teen participation in constructive and healthy activities that exclude drug use with the hope that these activities will offset the attraction to drugs. Examples of such activities include drug free dances, youth/adult leadership activities, community drop-in centers, and community service activities.

Among the community organizations that offer drug prevention programs are the following:

Boys and Girls Clubs of America. Located in every state, this private, nonprofit agency serves more than 4 million children and young adults at their more than 3,400 club locations. More than twenty-five national programs are available in the areas of education, the environment, health, the arts, careers, alcohol/drug and pregnancy prevention, gang prevention, leadership development, and athletics.

D.A.R.E. (Drug Abuse Resistance Education). A school-based prevention program, D.A.R.E. uses trained police officers to teach youth and teachers about the dangers of drug abuse.

National Youth Anti-Drug Media Campaign. Part of the Office of National Drug Control Policy, the organization targets youth ages nine to eighteen. It uses a variety of modern communications techniques, including advertising, public relations, and interactive media, as well as after-school programs to educate youth about the dangers of substance abuse.

A POLICE OFFICER TALKS TO STUDENTS ABOUT THE D.A.R.E. PROGRAM.

Living a drug-free life is a choice open to all young people. They are more likely to make that choice if there are exciting but safe opportunities to explore the world open to them. After-school programs that focus on developing teens' natural talents and interests, such as sports, theater, and music, empowering youth to choose safer, more positive alternatives to using drugs. As the medical, social, and legal risks of using these substances become better known and accepted by young people, the hope is that fewer and fewer will succumb to the lure of drug abuse and addiction in the future.

GLOSSARY

acid: Nickname for LSD.

addiction: A pattern of behavior based on great physical and/or psychological need for a substance or activity. Addiction is characterized by compulsion, loss of control, and continued repetition of a behavior no matter what the consequences.

angel dust: Common name for PCP.

anxiety: Uneasiness, worry, uncertainty, and fear that come with thinking about an anticipated danger which may be a normal reaction to a real threat or occur when no danger exists.

blotter acid: Sheets of absorbent paper soaked in LSD and dried. The most common form of LSD.

dependence: A physiological or psychological need for and craving for a particular substance, especially a drug.

dopamine: A neurotransmitter, or chemical messenger, in the brain that is affected by hallucinogens which the chemicals in hallucinogens affect as to the amount and action.

endorphin: A neurotransmitter that helps to elevate mood and alleviate pain, and which has receptors for heroin and other opiates.

ergot: A fungus that grows on rye and other grains.

flashback: An element of an LSD trip that recurs, sometimes long after all other effects of the drug have worn off.

glutamate: A neurotransmitter associated with pain, memory, and response to changes in the environment.

hallucination: Seeing, hearing, or feeling things that are not really there.

hallucinogens: A group of drugs that affect the central nervous system, producing a variety of vivid sensations and altering moods and thoughts.

HPPD: Hallucinogen persisting perception disorder; the spontaneous and sometimes continuous recurrence of perceptual effects of LSD long after an individual has ingested the drug.

ketamine: Dissociative anesthetic abused for its mind-altering effects and sometimes used to facilitate sexual assault.

locus coeruleus: Region of the brain that receives and processes sensory signals from all areas of the body.

lysergic acid diethylamide: The chemical name for LSD.

neurons: Nerve cells, the basic units of the nervous system, that are able to conduct impulses and communicate by releasing and receiving chemical messengers called neuro-transmitters.

neurotransmitters: Chemicals released by neurons (including serotonin, dopamine, adrenalin) that act to send nerve signals. When an imbalance among these chemicals occur, emotion and physical symptoms result.

PCP: Phencyclidine, a dissociative anesthetic abused for its mind-altering effects.

psychedelic: Relating to hallucinations or specifically to the LSD experience.

schizophrenia: Psychological disease characterized by mental confusion and sometimes associated with hearing voices.

serotonin: A neurotransmitter found in the brain and body that is involved in behavior, mood, memory, and appetite.

synapse: The gap between the nerve endings of two neurons. For a message to pass across the synapse, it needs help from a neurotransmitter.

tolerance: A condition in which a drug user needs increasing amounts of a drug to achieve the same level of intoxication once obtained from using smaller amounts.

FURTHER INFORMATION

Books

Algeo, Phillipa. *Acid and Hallucinogens.* New York: Franklin Watts, 1990.

Barter, James. *Hallucinogens.* San Diego, CA: Lucent Books, 2002.

Connolly, Sean. *Just the Facts: LSD.* Chicago: Reed Educational, 2001.

Hofmann, A. *LSD: My Problem Child.* New York: McGraw-Hill, 1980.

Lee, Martin, and Bruch Shlain. *Acid Dreams: The CIA, LSD, and the Sixties Rebellion.* Grove Press, 1986.

Littell, Mary Ann. *The Drug Library: LSD.* Springfield, NJ: Enslow Publishers, 1996.

Kuhn, Cynthia, Scott Scwartzwelder, and Wilkie Wilson. *Buzzed: The Straight Facts about the Most Abused Drugs from Alcohol to Ecstasy.* New York: W.W. Norton& Company, 2003.

Kuhn, Cynthia, Scott Swartzwelder, and Wilkie Wilson. *Just Say Know: Talking with Kids about Drugs and Alcohol.* New York: W.W. Norton & Company, 2002.

Project MKULTRA: The CIA's Program of Research in Behavioral Modification. Washington, D.C., Government Printing Office, August 31, 1977.

Medical Surveys

Centers for Disease Control and Prevention. *Youth Risk Behavior Surveillance—United States, 2003.* May 2004.

National Institute on Drug Abuse and University of Michigan. *Monitoring the Future National Survey Results on Drug Use, 1975-2003.* 2004.

U.S. Sentencing Commission. *2002 Sourcebook of Federal Sentencing Statistics.* 2004.

Medical Journals

Aghajanian, G. K., and Marek, G. J. Serotonin and hallucinogens. *Neuropsychopharmacology* 21: 16S-23S, 1999.

Backstrom, J. R., Chang, M. S., Chu, H., Niswender, C. M., and Sanders-Bush, E. Agonist-directed signaling of serotonin 5-HT2c receptors: differences between serotonin and lysergic acid diethylamide (LSD). *Neuropsychopharmacology* 21: 77S-81S, 1999.

Carroll, M. E. PCP and hallucinogens. *Advances in Alcohol and Substance Abuse* 9(1-2): 167-190, 1990.

Christophersen, A. S. Amphetamine designer drugs: an overview and epidemiology. *Toxicology Letters* 112-113: 127-131, 2000.

Javitt, D. C., and Zukin, S. R. Recent advances in the phency-clidine model of schizophrenia. *American Journal of Psychiatry* 148:1301-1308, 1991.

Web Sites

Alateen
www.al-anon.org
A twelve-step recovery program for young people designed "to help families and friends" of alcoholics recover from the effects of living with the problem drinking of a relative or friend. Its program of recovery is adapted from Alcoholics Anonymous and is based upon the Twelve Steps, Twelve Traditions, and Twelve Concepts of Service. Since many alcoholics also abuse other drugs, this site, and the Alateen program, may help drug abusers address their problem.

Partnership for a Drug Free America
www.drugfreeamerica.org
This nonprofit, private organization provides information about steroids and other substances on its Web site. It offers pages just for parents as well as a kid-friendly question-and-answer page.

National Clearinghouse for Alcohol and Drug Information (NCADI)
www.ncadi.samhsa.gov/
P.O. Box 2345
Rockville, MD 20847-2345
Phone: 800-729-6686

INDEX

ABOUT THE AUTHOR

Suzanne LeVert is the author of more than twenty-five young adult and adult nonfiction titles. She specializes in health and medical subjects as well as the social sciences. Ms. LeVert has written five books in the Marshall Cavendish Benchmark *Drugs* series. Born in Natick, Massachusetts, Ms. LeVert now practices law in New Orleans, Louisiana, where she comes face to face with the legal and social problems caused by illegal drug addiction and trafficking.